User Manual for
Literate Human Kind

User Manual for Literate Human Kind

J . A . THOMAS

PARTRIDGE
A Penguin Random House Company

To order additional copies of this book, contact
Partridge India
000 800 10062 62
orders.india@partridgepublishing.com

www.partridgepublishing.com/india

Acknowledgement

First and foremost I thank the Lord.

I am thankful for the support of late Adv. G John and Mirsha K Ayoob.

I thank my parents Mr. C. T Abraham and Laila Abraham for the motivation in publishing this book and thank my sister Annu Abraham for the mental support in all fields.

I also thank Mr. Ashish T.J, who helped me to a lot.

A special thanks to Mr. K P Prajit Kumar and Mr. George Varghese for their continued support.

A sincere thanks to Mr. Nitin Thomas **(EDITOR)** *for building my confidence and making this book a one to look forward to.*

I would like to express my gratitude to Miss Yanessa Evans and Miss Ann Minoza (Partridge Publishing) for helping me solve all problems from the 1st step in publishing this book. I am also appreciable for their greatness of mind.

J.A. Thomas

I am deeply grateful to Mr. Deepak Joseph Potanaani, Mr. Jaseem Muhammed, Mr. Bibin Benjamin George, Mr Sameer Bava and Mr. Mahesh. V. Menon for the motivation I have enjoyed in successfully completing this book.

I would like to give a quick thanks to Mr X and Mr Y whose names are being with held for their kindness I have enjoyed.

And finally I am thankful to all my Friends and Relatives who have been with me and supported me, in my journey called "LIFE"

"Peace Is TheFuel for the System"

"Be Good To Others, So They Will Be Good To You"

"Patience Leads To Prevention of System Overload"

"System Support Is the Outcome of Peace Production"

"Nobody Should Be the Cause of Others Sufferings"

"Infinite Lines Can Be Drawn Through the Same Point"

"Respect Is Something You Need To Give In-Order to Get It Back"

R

Introduction:

System includes every object enjoying the gravity of THE EARTH.

As a human being, what the system requires from us is the fuel to run the system. If we provide enough fuel for the system, it will run faster.

Faster does not mean days will be shorter. Faster refers to faster development.

What is development?

"selah"

Development is the process of the system, which increases the comfort of a human being

Ex: *"If people were giving enough fuel for the system before the invention of the bulb. They would have got it even before it was actually found".*

Earlier invented, earlier it reaches the common man.

For generations, after the invention of the bulb it became a major tool against darkness. The masses kept upgrading it and it is being upgraded even now.

The comfort it has been giving to the people is in great effect.

Understanding the system with a single subject is very difficult.

The system can do wonders if you keep feeding fuel.

ARISE; let us generate *(1) fuel for the SYSTEM. *(1) *(The fuel is PEACE).*

At first Generating peace will be a difficult task, but once you get to generating it, it will show how the system supports you and will carry you forward. This is how miracles happen.

Another law people should understand:

L1: **"In the System Infinite Lines Can Be Drawn through the Same Point".**

In our day-to-day life, the point is a scenario and the lines drawn are every persons view and its projections drawn through it.

This helps to makes each person, *(2) unique from each other. *(2) *(The uniqueness is the law of the system).*

A person's needs too play a big role, in making him/her unique.

The system needs you to look at it with a view, where the projection is for peace.

When Oneness/Unity of the units in the system is to achieve cent percent into the view of peace, then everyone gains and no loss is involved.

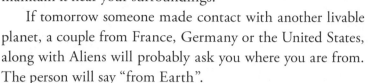

Even though there is no need to go to the extremes, at least maintain it near your surroundings.

If tomorrow someone made contact with another livable planet, a couple from France, Germany or the United States, along with Aliens will probably ask you where you are from. The person will say "from Earth".

When the oneness of peace is implemented, then the system goes faster, or tomorrow people will have to go from here to some other place, to find His/her living.

Ex: *Like people in India, going to the Middle East to make their living.*

There will most assuredly be an inconvenience of adjustment.

So come on guy's fuel up, work for it, achieve it and let's speed up our system.

It's how you relate your thoughts. If your thoughts generate peace, which is the fuel of the system, then the [3] system requires you. [3] *(Richness)*

Once the system requires you, it will show a growth in you. In the Bible there is a verse where Jesus says:

v1: *"Those who work for the [4] will of my father are my brothers, sisters and mothers".* [4] *(refers to generating fuel/peace)*

At first, start working for it in your close circle where you belong.

Once you start working for it, there will be a step where you will realize that the system works wonders in you and you enjoy happiness around you.

When there is happiness around you, your life becomes easier, and you start thinking creatively which the system supports.

The objectives of all religions are the same; it's to make people generate peace, the fuel to the system.

In a music track there is a phrase which says "You see all what you need to see". The system needs peace. Make it need peace or an opportunity to generate the same.

What the system wants is "what you need to generate", that has to be the basic motto of mankind. 100 Billion Wind mills can generate more power than 20 nuclear reactors, if and only if wind is present and the direction is in accordance with the winds direction. Hence, wind is the system support.

This is how we need to generate. Every human being has to be a unique unit, which can provide the system with fuel. Opportunities are present in every level of the system.

"selah"

If Oneness is present in every creature under the atmosphere, the system runs faster.

If your thoughts and doings generate fuel to the system, then you can overcome fear and tension, which can harm anything under the atmosphere until he/she transfers it into useful energy which is productive, and in return you need to maintain the balance in a mutual way.

E

A satisfactory deal is when everyone dealing with it is happy, which is a byproduct of peace. This is one of the reasons, the rich are getting richer and the poor are getting poorer.

They (the poor) need to maintain their view of peace which is the direction of your windmill. They are travelling in a different direction, and need to turn accordingly.

Richness is a feeling you get, when you realize that the system needs you.

The utilisation of opportunities by a human being in every level is the reason for their growth. Reaching that level which generates peace is because of their thoughts and doings. The more you generate, the more you get closer to being rich. The value of a unit is directly proportional to the value of system support he/she has received, and receiving as a result of peace generation.

Relativeness does matter a lot in your work for peace. Everything in this world is limited by your senses, till you die.

When compared to a computer, our Eyes, Nose, Ears and Touch are the input units. The Tongue is an output unit.

"selah"

Neglecting the other input unit which is also very important. Here, input refers to the input directly connected to the brain. Any unit which produces comparatively good output will be related to "**As Good**".

Jesus Christ has told:

v2: *"For every kind of beast and bird, of reptile and sea creature, can be tamed and has been tamed by mankind but no human being can tame the tongue. It is a restless evil, full of deadly poison".*

We must train it or at least give it a try. Rules have its own limitations; kindly make it fearless, for people to live in the corresponding area. If Development happens, life will be much happier and easier.

Even if things are not easy i.e. having difficulty adapting/ adjusting; from the people who are working and generating, some among them are always remembered.

It is "**Situations**" that make people go against it.

If the objective is a satisfactory deal then keep thinking, there will most definitely be a way out.

Make sure that you are not being ruled by just paper.

People, who don't have to break a sweat for emergency necessities, can help some to balance their survival.

Help at-least the ones you come across. If you think he/she is lacking in generating peace, support them, and lead them in the right direction to overcome fear.

"Kindness" and *"Generosity"* are always given a thumbs up by the system.

As a result people will be happier and let evolution happen faster.

Ex: *Buying a comb from a shop helps adding a drop more in atleast 3 family's account.*

Promote them give them **motivation**.

Tongue is the output unit so be careful when *[5] outputting *[5] *(talking)*.

When you relate "**The Tongue**" with other sense organs, the latter can only be manipulated to a limit.

Make sure that the output is being delivered, after thinking in at least 2 angles. The 2 angles can be increased over the period of time. As has been told before, you can draw infinite number of lines through the same point *(L1)*.

If steps taken are always for peace then go ahead, Proceed. When Governments, religions and every human work for peace, then our objective in this world is complete till the beginning of limitless life.

This is the time, let us work for peace.

Work as one, no matter what the colour of your skin, or religion, our goal is "being a human with productivity." Fear depends on how you project things. **"Fear"** and **"Ego"** are the weapons of the opposition.

"selah"

Fear can be overcome by knowing about the limit.

Ex: *When a family is late catching a bus for going on vacation, the wife has a doubt whether she has switched off the gas stove. She remembered it, while traveling on the bus to the railway station.*

Any direction or projection you give or send through that point doesn't amount to anything as her peace is lost because of this waste of currency, which in turn cannot be resolved without the help of another unit.

If she needs to get out of it, she needs support from the people around.

"Happiness is the byproduct of peace". "Harmony also has a role in being a byproduct".

A

Not every Invention can be a hit, but others are always a spark for the rest to develop or to attain greater heights.

Opportunities are everywhere, with an experience you can gain for having in limitless life.

Experiences are not your experiences alone, but of other's too. It can be either past or present. Present is always better, due to the fact that it helps the system to give you enough knowledge you need, other than your academics.

Every Individual needs to get knowledge from the system, which will help them to build it up. That knowledge you get is related to your "**karma**".

"selah"

When you get knowledge from the shared experiences, the system does not need to give you a chance for repetitive understanding.

Your presence in a pleasant and productive way in others situation is highly appreciated, and the system support you as favor.

This sharing of burden will help you generate peace.

As an output unit, the tongue has the power to make the brain to act accordingly. So if you see a couple of projections before the role of the tongue, you can control it to some extent.

If the tongue produces peace, your body automatically supports it, and you get a byproduct of the energy conversion which is "**happiness and harmony**". That's what you deserve.

Alcohol magnifies your projections for the time being. These projections are caused due to our own tongue, or someone else's output.

To people who see only the **sunset**; BE IT KNOWN, there is always a **sunrise**, only thing is that it's on the other side. The peace generators keep magnifying their projections after booze. That's the reason major religions cannot limit the use of it.

One, who can generate or support a group, can have some money for his/her luxury. He/she demands it. It's only when they change their direction of thought/*(6) perception *(6) *(projection)*, they start to fall. The higher you are the farther you will fall, when the direction is changed.

So People, let's all make things faster.

Ex: *When Britain Invaded Major part of the world, they were the most developed.*

Rather than fighting and wasting our time. Let's develop, only then will we have future.

Controlling the *(7) output unit *(7) *(tongue),* can give you a great opportunity to think. Thinking is the capacity of a human being to build creativity, by adding on different dimensions.

Ex: *If Newton and his friend were sitting below the apple tree and apple fell when they were talking about a lady in the neighborhood. The situation would be the same but his invention (result due to the projection), would not be activated.*

A

Based on the fact, he was sitting alone without using his output until he was able to think about the reason why it fell and started building up and progressing, his thoughts made him find reason, to why it fell.

L2: **Just like the bending of light when passing through glass or any medium having higher molecular density**, the waves/outputs produced from human being can be bended by another *(8) human being *(8) (*unit*) by relating it to a situation, keeping every unit as a medium.

How ever advanced a computer system may be, the output is obtained only if there is an input. It's only when the output of the person close to you is *(9) good *(9) (*peace*), will your input also depend on it.

Both the input and the output are co-related.

L3: **Every action has an equal and opposite reaction**. Sharing our burden with each other, is the biggest *(10) satisfactory deal *(10) (*positive*) with the system. If thinking from systems point of view.

The uniqueness of an individual is due to his/her needs. Many think the burden is due to wealth. Majority is, but, there is at least some which doesn't involve the afore-mentioned, which could be solved just by ideas. All you need is to share and solve it.

Knowledge about the limits, are highly essential for generating peace. Every situation is created by relating the equations with relativity of:

- Time
- Distance (from your place/landmark)
- Speed
- Venue
- No. of people

In all these cases some standard units are used for our calculation benefit.

Your thoughts/Perception is work of your brain. So it is computed using the laws of relativity.

9/10 is good
9/25 is neutral and
9/50 is fail.

So 9 is a constant while, what we relate depends on the output.

If 9 is the truth, it's how you relate to the situation. Every individual is a sophisticated unit of the system.

Diseases are complex patterns produced by your brain, which causes difference in the usual cycles of your body.

Good byproducts will be absent, if the main product is bad.

L4: **Parallel lines never collide**. Collision always produces energy loss. To make the system efficiency to the maximum, we need to reduce energy wastage.

As people, we need to attain oneness in our objective. It's hard to think of everyone having the same objective. "selah"

Your family is a unit. Thereby, with respect to all units in a family, you are not a single unit anymore, if the unit maintains a cumulative peace in and out[11]

[11] (*here unit refers to family, be it inside or outside your home. Then the output is fuel, supporting each individual in that unit (family).*

Ex: A magnet never attaches itself to iron; likewise, you can enjoy its byproducts, namely "**Harmony**" and "**Happiness**".

Things getting solved on its own or you finding new options, is an indication of your good productivity. Every religion tries to convey this message to the common folk.

D

It's all how *things *(*inputs*) are taken or "**The Attitude**".

Anger is a process where there is a lot of energy wastage, which is not appreciated by the system.

You don't have an option to change the past, even if it's a wastage caused due to any reason whatsoever. The system doesn't like to waste anymore energy on it, so think of the next option with minimum wastage.

Everything is a chain reaction of the system. When a person's output is good/ fuel generating, it's a good input for the people around. "Your output and doings depend on how you think".

Family as a unit with good productivity of parents is highly influential on the direction of productivity for their children. In this book *(12) productivity *(12) (*refers to as production of peace/ fuel*).

You may be of any religion, country or continent, the objective of rules and traditions, are for increasing the productivity of units in it and maintaining the balance with the system.

As an individual maintain the peace around you, share the burden of people around as much as possible.

The needs of units are different in different levels of the hierarchy, set by the system.

Ex: **His/her burden won't be a day's meal's expense or a vacation of 2 days of a unit, in higher levels of hirarchy**.

At least give hope to the suffering, and make him/her think in the right direction.

Money is just a medium which flows through the places, where productivity is high. In order to increase the flow of the medium we need to be open. To find the limits, you need to explore.

"**Unity is power**", it's the energy of people in it (unity). The rest of energy required for accomplishment of the goal is given from the system, if the unity is for production/satisfactory deal.

Nothing in this world is evil if the direction of your projection is for oneness, productivity or sharing of burden. Share your food with the hungry, eventually your hunger will subsidize, thinking of the fuel productivity. Adjusting is easier, if you generate and prioritize the objective.

Disease is the mechanism of eliminating the impurities and cleaning up the system in order to maintain its balance, so don't be a part of it. "**Fear is friction; overcome it, while learning to balance**".

Don't think earth is the only planet where life existed or exists. It's only the method of transport, which blocks our way to reach the others.

What do you prefer? Making them work for you or you are working for *[13] them *[13] (*Aliens*). Evolve into a more developed and literate citizen, tune your projection for better clarity.

There are people who have committed suicides for a few thousands. Aren't they in need? When prioritized or related with lack of food, war, people don't focus on them. When people broaden their minds they see options, which also demands focus. Only when more people focus on it, will you find that there will be similar categories in different levels of the hierarchy in the system.

What is a standard product?

Any product which makes the job of the user easiest to do, has high efficiency, speed, reliability, can make the user most comfortable and has a value in the society is considered a standard product.

An individual's standard is shown by the care given to his/her personal things.

Relate with the comforts of the other fuel generators, so your happiness is boosted by the generation of peace.

The effect of your *(14) doings *(14) *(Sharing burden)* reduces, when you use the output unit for your doings to the other units.

"**People wakeup**", don't fight for the scraps in another's plate. There are a lot of dishes in the menu of the system, all your need is to know it, the richness you need to achieve it and work for it. Let this vision be for peace to you and others around you.

Wealth may accumulate in some people, depending on how important he/she is to the system. There is no point fighting for it, without doing your part.

W

Once you realize your importance in and to the system, then you can overcome fear by testing its limit.

Astrology is the study of influence of parts of system, in the characteristics of human. Parts of the system in Indian Astrology, is the influence of planets, sun and moon.

The relation with the planetary positions at that point of time and at that latitude and longitude is taken. In western Astrology stars and constellations as a part of the system, to relate to the character of a person is used.

All these calculations can be edited by the system, depending on his/her productivity. The richness is always the effect of faith and production of fuel with the system support.

The "**Us Theory**" is the reason for vengeance, terrorism and everything against peace, but when the **Us Theory** works for all mankind, the System can do wonders.

Today the technology is so advanced that people can work for oneness easily. Remove all worries, produce fuel and move ahead.

Talk less about the favors you have done, so the system can favor you more.

"**Developed Countries**", upgrade your productivity and help the developing to develop faster. Do not worry about your destruction, all that happens is equilibrium where everyone gains, even the systems gains and grows powerful/faster.

The developing country should not fear that *(15) they *(15)(*developed countries*) will over power you. The oneness objectives can destroy the fear easily.

Your limitful/limited life may be for a century, even if you produce less, don't waste energy in fighting each other.

Traditions have their own limits, as the environment changes rapidly and traditions are not viable for such rapidity. Environment changes from day to day rapidly. There are many restrictions that they try to fit in the present day environment.

Its only when it is seen from the 2nd persons view, alterations/ updates are made. The 1st person is a group and it's leaders. There may be accidents but keep it balanced, so that minimum harm occurs.

"**Observe**", there are answers around you for your questions.

In the system there will be similar problems in many levels and the system has its mechanism to solve it. If you observe you can find it, as that is what you are looking for. A single person's minor problems may be another person's major one.

OR

"A little act from one's end can lead to huge impact".

Cut a tree, but make sure that you have planted and taken care of one for the future, while finding a mutual balance with the system. Those who have found it should help the others to find it. All you need is to open, discusses and find the solution which produces maximum fuel for the system.

"**Ego**" and "**Fear**" which cause worry are the opposite reactions of peace.

Rather than adjusting your projection to collide with the one you are relating to, it's always better to make a parallax in their direction. Find a step to move ahead with your competitor. Work for your productivity.

Forgive others not because they deserve forgiveness, but you deserve peace –

A bad incident, feels better when you comparing it with a worse one. What's happened is happened you cannot change it, so don't waste more energy on it, move on.

"selah"

R

Making a peaceful environment is always an additive for increasing the number of inventions. The better the environment, the faster the invention. Things that actually make the user comfortable will become a hit, and the rest is for its up gradation in the future. When people feel their richness, their fear subsides in them.

Get to the right direction through a point, the rest is the work of the system.

In order to understand the system you need to observe it.

The unavailability of objective with the system by a group/organization/civilization is the reason for its perishing.

This book is written in English because it's the only language known to me in which the meaning doesn't change much in accordance with the tone of delivery of the sentence.

Even then, there will still be a classification in the group. It is not a mistake; it's a mechanism of the system to promote the units with good productivity.

Believe in what you believe, only faith and objective does matter. Beware of fear and worries which are the friction for your productivity. Generating peace and creating oneness is your objective as a human. Rules and laws have their limits, as they cannot have a live relation with the situation. All you have to do is to give the highest priority to the option, which you consider will generate most peace.

This has to be parallel to the law, so the law has to be updated to the present day conditions.

Every human being is needy but their needs are different.

L5: **Science is a tool to understand the creations, and the laws of the system**. So they help us to advance, in knowing the creations.

Involve and Evolve are two rhyming words, which has a great bond in between.

Before you take a decision, make sure that it doesn't hurt anyone. You can convey your point in various ways, without hurting anyone.

For some people, even their appreciation does hurt.

Ex: **Great Britain had colonies all over the world, but their defeat was the result of the unity of native people in a country/colony without considering caste, religion etc**. They were supported by the system. This colonization was a mechanism of the system, to increase their unity.

Development of this unity can prevent the same situations arising in our planet by others outside in future.

The "**Unity**" and "**Sophistication**" equipped with us, before they visit, can at least move them into considering us as equals.

We may be separated from each other by water, ocean or maybe even mountains. Still, we are all a part of same circle/sphere.

Sadness/Grief is also a mechanism of the system, to give you some knowledge from the system, by the system to overcome fear. Its knowledge and experience, which you will most probably use, even after your limitful life.

Divide and Rule is the method implemented for maximum output of management. It has a relation or similarity to the Nuclear Fission Reaction. But it can be controlled by limiting, the number of neutrons in the nuclear plant.

On the other hand, there is hundred times more output energy in nuclear fusion reaction.

Fusion is the reaction, where the molecules combine and produce energy.

Here combinations of molecules are only what matters.

This combination depends on the availability of molecules of the similar category.

If we refer ourselves as molecules, the similar category refers to the ones with same objective.

If at 1st, someone joins the latter for helping the former. Along with the 1st person's option you are adding the 2nd ones too, for the same situation.

Some of the 2nd person's option may fall in the same category as with the 1st, even then he can go through the 2nd person's option, to get the maximum productivity by the relation of the same, in a situation.

There are happier ways to convey the sad news. Just relate with worse.

Science is a tool for exploring nature and creation, along with mathematics.

"selah"

It's a tool to explore, not just to work for someone.

I

Once you get the richness and have your objective set, you will slowly realize that whatever you do, it will generate peace.

Like **Sacrifice**, "**forgiveness**" is also a tool for generating peace.

In the system, a mechanism of transferring information/data's is present. By the law of nature not everyone has the same capacity, so target your maximum productivity. Set the highest priority for your productivity.

Think before you speak, your output is another's input.

Have faith in what you believe.

Appreciate the people for their work, so that the rest are motivated.

Life is a complexity of simple things, it's how you take it and build on it.

When someone doesn't need something, there are millions who need it, boiling down to the reach you have and "**technology**" can help you increase your reach.

L6: **Unity in diversity is a law of the system**. As written above, the diversity on numerical 9/10, 9/25 and 9/50 refers to, It's how you put the value in the denominator.

"Patience" is a key part for the objective.

According to the system you are a packet of data, or a unit which carries data.

"Virginity" holds the key to the availability for exploring another level or layer of carnal pleasure, which deviates from the subject, you were thinking till then.

"Generosity" holds the key to start your unit.

"Honesty" is related to the objective of the organization.

"Education" is the process to project the future generation, in the right direction.

T

Which light wave has maximum power?

Laser light travels the farthest, and is the most powerful light form.

The specialty of laser is that every wave is parallel to each other, which is due to prevention of collision between the rays.

The problem with this world at present, is wastage of energy due to increased collisions, which in turn results in a lesser efficient system.

What we can infer from "**Collision**" is that, when a person puts his/her projection through a point and a group supports him/her, then the strength of the group, depends on the number of people with the same direction of the projection.

When people with the same objective increase and they all belong to the same group, this is when a group becomes stronger.

If the group adds productivity, then there is always support from the system.

When we realize the objectives and working of the system, the system need not make us suffer, in order for us to receive data's.

Be it may, whatever happens, the system will give you data's/information that you need to transport to other units, or in your limitless life.

So you'd better get it, by helping someone.

If we maintain the balance of the system, then it's time to evolve and help the system, to **make it a better place**.

Complexion or colour of a human being is just our property to visualize "**Reflected Light**", but that person's "**Inner Light**" is limited by your senses.

There is everything required for everyone in the system to survive, the problem only being that, it is scattered here and there. But the opposition has been made into groups and they fight for it for survival.

The oneness feel will only come, when you visit someone else's place and meet a neighbor.

Thus work for it, get it developed. It's only when we are weak/fragile, the voice for our feelings are never heard.

Otherwise our future generations, will suffer like our past ones.

You tend to go to a place which satisfies your requirement, only when your native environment doesn't provide you with what you need. To maintain the unity there are other torrid ways for the system, why should we be sadists.

Combine our technologies as a defense against aliens and be equipped, which is doable and the system will wonderfully support you.

Once you get the tool, start exploring even though you can't make a revolution. You can however make a point, through which infinite lines can pass in either the present or in the future.

Accumulating wealth is not a mistake, but make sure that you don't hurt anyone and that none of your neighbors are suffering for imagine, a 10% of your income. "**Transportation**" is the spine for development. Develop and earn money the right way. Support him even when he is only supported by the system.

"**Observation**" is the key of finding opportunity. Don't suffer, just adjust.

The Us Concept keeps changing, in accordance with the openness of your mind.

"**Less wastage more efficiency**", that's what the system requires.

Peace generation will and can make the world, a good place to live.

"**Music**" is a language of expressing emotions; it can produce various emotions, due to the fact that you "**Relate**" your thoughts to the tone you have already registered in your mind, knowingly or unknowingly.

The Music which gives you peace and energy are the ones which activate your relativeness with the old one already in your subconscious mind, in order to increase your creativity.

It's all how you prioritize, give the highest priority for peace generation, then the fear gets eliminated, and once fear is eliminated you get confidence.

"selah"

When the direction is right and you have gained confidence, then is the time to begin a unit called family.

World as an entity is also called the system.

Even a bacteria or a virus has its role in it.

Any planetary object becomes a star and grows, due to the fusion reaction.

The advantages of stars are that, the access by foreign bodies are low and is a standard for atleast a few planets.

Think about your decisions made previously and measure your output, then decide on a better option the next time you make a decision in a similar situation. As a result you can relate with that and can thus make a point you can use, in similar situations in various levels of your life.

Upgrade your productivity; increase your capacity for absorbing the burden of others, which is the objective.

"selah"

Unity is power, it's not to use against the same kind of unit of a similar category in the system.

The visual of the unit is due to which units adapt, but understand that you are handicapped or limited by your eyes to see the inner light.

Situations make people take decisions; the capacity of that person to overcome the opposite energy and take the right decision in the right direction, is what increases his/her richness.

Everything depends on patience, for the system to process the reward of your output. Don't wait idle, in the meantime keep producing and let the cycle continue.

Ex: Rather than that, **keep outputting unwanted pop-ups like you are browsing on an unprotected computer**.

Process the input for better and faster output, which is required by the system.

"**Man proposes, God disposes**", this is because either the direction is wrong or the system has better plans for you. Another reason being, relating to a future point where your direction of present proposal will collide.

Or else the system should approve the proposal.

When you are protected by the system, nothing *(16) unwanted *(16) *(inputs/data's)* comes to you.

Analyze your productivity and increase it by working on it, at the same time keep an observation around you and keep your input units open, to relate with the situations you may face at a later stage. Analyze, relate and create a point in your mind and work on it.

"**Keep calm, keep cool**".

Life is not a race, even though you are sitting on the bed surfing the web, be it known that you are moving in various directions.

It's not a race; it's a set of units moving in the same direction with informations of the system.

Extinction is the cause of a deadlock situation with lots of energy wastage.

Even though you travel extensively, it's not even 1% of the distance you have travelled along with the system. In every rotation, your environment keeps changing and things around you also change.

So get the richness and support of the system get equipped.

Uniqueness is maintained in the system due to the points he/she had been in and the points he/she has yet to be in. All that matters is just the direction of your decisions at these points.

Wealth is a medium which increases your confidence. It is also equipment for raising other's confidence level too.

Increase your resistance towards the opposite force.

If you calculate the amount of money and the space used on a built fence, shelter and food can be provided for the ones who don't have it.

Support the system and get supported by it, then break the barriers and overcome fear.

Growth of both fear and ego are always chain reactions. If it gets into you, produce more so that you get more support and tools from the system, to destroy it.

If there is wastage, try to collect it and reuse it productively.

Understand the needs of others, if it is not too much to ask for, help him/her to achieve theirs.

It's not how much wealth you accumulate, its how much capacity you have, to generate.

If someone finds a fault with another and expresses it in a non- productive way, then the latter will most assuredly find a fault with the former.

Be with the system, when you are in it.

More importance is given for the packing than for the product, it is because you are being limited by your senses.

Everything happens for a reason, which is the result of education by the system.

My observation of people, who were able to perform miracles, was an after effect of limitful life, a coma or such kind of things.

It is because limitless life is being touched by them, even when their input and output units are shut.

Opposing forces will be there and has to be present, for the working of the system.

Even though friction is a cause of energy wastage, we need it to walk; the only thing is it should be minimized.

Keep the objective constant and change your life style, in accordance to the environment you are living in.

Benefit yourself, but not while others in the deal suffer.

Old ones retire and advocate the young, to work for the progress.

In a developing or developed economy there is a saying, **"the rich get richer and the poor get poorer"**.

This is because of *(17) their *(17)(*rich*) right direction of projection, and the output of these units produced will give a higher support to the system, so system supports him/her.

As the 1st step, poor people set your direction in the right way for maximum output.

For those who are generating, upgrade and help the others who support the system.

Since you have got support from the system, which is the result of your productivity you need to support people whose needs can be achieved just by you, with or without much effort.

Quality of a person depends on his/her output and decisions at a point, which results in maximum productivity.

Attitude of a person depends on the relation with the 2nd person and his/her reputation.

When that 2nd person tells you about someone's attitude, you need to relate the relation between them.

If the respective attitude is bad to the 2nd person, it doesn't necessarily mean that it has to be the same with you.

E

People go in an opposite direction, when they fear the consequences of going in the right direction, hence they are illiterate about the support of the system, if it's in the right direction.

Overcome both fear and worry, when going in the right direction.

Life is a rally along with the system where each inner unit, learn and improve on how to avoid collisions.

It's more like the deal, i.e. "**Support the System – System Will Support you**".

"selah"

"**Fear**" and "**Worry**" is the friction which you need, to a limit.

Either the system will help you overcome it, or its better you try to extend your limits.

Wealth is the mechanism of the system to increase your confidence, until it creates a fear due to an excess of the same.

The situation of fear due to excess wealth is created, when there is a projection in an inefficient direction.

The aim has to be for oneness of units in the system. It can be worked to a greater extent, when the objective is parallel to the systems.

The "**Right Decision**" is where maximum *(18) productivity *(18) (*generating peace*) occurs among the "**Possible Options**".

Relation of peace and invention can be explained as follows: Invention is the result of creative thinking and creative thinking is the result of your peace of mind.

When there are a lot of unwanted inputs, even though it is processed by the mind, they are all the deviations of creative thinking.

Set the objective, help the rest to achieve the same and achieve richness.

Make the system perfect and enjoy the perfection around you.

Anyone working for peace remains and survives with harmony, as the system requires it, for them.

Faith is directly proportional to richness.

Your imagination has its limits, as you are limited by the mass. We have explored only less than 5% of the Milky Way; there are a lot more galaxies which we are limited to, due to our body being in this system.

Ex: **In some parts of the world, when 3 trains go through, below or above the road so that cars don't get stuck waiting for it, and in some where people die smashing into trains without proper railway gate and in others where time and energy is wasted due to cars waiting for trains to pass.**

System needs monitoring of productivity and maintaining it, people consider it a race.

The amount of fuel generated is the one counted and recorded. That is what you gain in the certificate when you enter limitless life.

Sleep is the processing time for the mind, to process the projections in different directions, combinations and storage of what input you have received the day before.

Adjustments are always supported by adaptation which is a mechanism of the system support, to do the satisfactory deal and get out for good.

It's not how many times you read the Holy Book, it's how much you understand the concepts correctly.

There are 60 muscles on your face; expressions are combinations of these muscles. Smile is the right combination of these muscles which can provide happiness to you and to the people around. Use these combinations in situations, where you give relief to others in situations which require you to do so.

Don't be a burden to others, in a deal where they are suffering and you can survive in the situation, without the benefit not affecting you for the day's survival.

Our access to the limitless life is limited till you die.

"**Generosity**" is the outcome as well as the symptom of richness.

If you have achieved richness help the others in achieving it, which automatically increases your achieved richness.

Doing bad things are always accompanied by the fear of doing good ; the truth you are ignorant about is the support from the system.

At the beginning everyone comes to this world as a blank CD or a pen drive. System feeds you with information in its every rotation and revolution.

It's how you use that information's, to combine and generate fuel for the system.

What you see and understand is the relation between the combinations of past, present and the environment you have been to.

"selah"

Experience won't be same for all people in the same situations; productivity has a major role in the support of the system in that particular situation, for every individual.

"Bravery is the result of richness".

"No one is your enemy, until one is set by you in your mind".

In the system no similar unit should fight.

Astrology is the classification of human kind on the basis of direction of projection, and is related to constant units around the system.

Any unit in any category can tune your direction for the objective, to achieve the support.

Survival of the fittest is outdated.

"Survive and help the rest to survive".

In the infinite lines drawn through a point, there are many lines which has productivity, in that the most productive are the most beneficial. Wealth is the medium which fills the area between you and the lower levels, hope is the rope you are clinging onto. The strength of your grip depends on your capacity of production. *Medium(*wealth) is a gel which looks rigid.

It is the medium to stand on after that situation, till you find the next rope.

Wealth keeps filling the gap when you cling onto hope.

Only if you have an umbrella can you help others or at least some under it, during rainfall.

So people try getting *(19) one *(19) (*umbrella*), if you have one, upgrade to something bigger or get another one.

Here umbrella refers to the equipments you are equipped with, for the production of peace.

Researchers keep working not against anyone in the system, but for making our system efficient.

Appreciate the system for the support, give thanks and work for increasing your productivity.

You are a part of the system; anyone in any field in the system has the capacity, to combine their knowledge to produce peace. Even the right combination of your facial muscles can generate peace to some extent.

The people who are making adjustments in a deal should not be ignored, they demand appreciation.

"Peace is always accompanied by harmony and happiness".

You don't have an eject button to end your limited life, all you have is a self destruct button where you have to evolve from a single celled organism, to reach your limitless life.

Every creature in the system is a unit with specifications like RAM, ROM etc. It's their capacity in which they survive, and which can get upgraded with system support.

A good update of a product keep the existing standard product get outdated, this is the mechanism of the system to make the product reached the units especially to those who cannot.

Do not let fear over power your mind.

Human beings are the only units in the system which can convert any energy to useful energy, but there will be some loss of energy during conversion which is a system law.

Some of the doctors treat patients, while majority work for the prevention of the disease.

Prevention is always better than cure.

Wealth issues can always happen, but know that it's not evenly distributed. Give the struggling whatever you have in excess, for your survival concept.

This doesn't mean don't take it back. Take it back when they are comfortable, it has a high productivity of peace.

People living in a developed place resist, in going and settling in a developing place.

This is because their local environment can meet the individual's requirement while the latter cannot.

Standardization of a livable area can help us, achieve this difference.

System has many ways of increasing the unity, Ex: **Everyone in a refugee camp is a natural calamity, but is also a way of the system.**

Development is the result of peace productivity of people living there; it also refers to the rule and law of the corresponding place.

A

Every law in system which has the power to maintain a continuous presence of peace around the environment where its limits are, are the best ones. Adapt it, upgrade it and put it around the system, for the constant production of peace by an individual.

Law is derived by relating traditions, infrastructure, and convenience for the rulers and for the common man.

This if appropriately kept, can suppress the presence of the opposition in the system.

So actively work on it, and find the best way to attain maximum productivity.

In comparison to the acceleration of development after the colonial period of time, it can be found that even though it varies within different countries, still it is multiplying 50 times faster.

When there is peace for the poor, which in turn gets you peace as a productive unit. Some time is given to the individual to think about something else, other than their burden.

The rich make requirements to the system, but the weak get tested.

Be proud to be a unit who generates peace, so you can/will be equipped with richness.

The weak clinch heavily to the rope of faith/hope, so that they can overcome fear.

When you enter the limitless life, all you are equipped with is the knowledge/data you are holding as a unit, and the unit of peace produced.

This is all you are allowed to take from this system, when you are being transferred to another stage.

If you are trying to press the self destruct button at any point in time, don't. If you destroy yourself make sure that it is always supported by the system, when the destruction is helping the survival of some individuals.

Suppress the opposite force, but if the opposition is richer, then there is a mistake in your projection.

When the 1st person is doing something nice to the 2nd person, the 2nd person may take it in a bad sense.

On the other hand, when the 1st person is doing something nice to the 2nd person and the 2nd person takes it in a good way, there is a production of fuel generation takes place.

"**Inventions**" are answers to the questions asked by the inventor to the system. At the time of asking, they were *[20] rich *[20] (*support by the system*), so the system answered their questions.

As an individual, generate as much you can at every moment, as the unit of measuring it is unknown to us.

Any system will become slower, when there is an increase in its load.

When the objective direction is the same as with the system, the light moving parallel to each ray has the maximum speed of travelling.

Every reaction needs more than an element/compound, but every element/compound has its own purpose in the reaction.

Meet the purpose and generate fuel as much as you can, whenever possible

When_biology is dissected to a deeper extent, it is found to be a combination of physics and chemistry accompanied by mathematics.

"selah"

Hence, everything around the system can be under stood with the same subjects as given above, i.e. physics, chemistry accompanied by mathematics.

The problem with us humans are, we often forget the fact that we are limited by our senses.

N

As data's travel in packets, we are also units carrying data travelling in packets. In a packet, the faster the unit reaching the front of a packet in a moving direction, the quicker they can enjoy peace as there are minimal obstacles in the front row, and no one blocks your vision.

What everyone targets is that peace, when they are right in front of the packet/group of units.

This packet become more efficient when every single unit in the packet reaches at a similar time, for this to happen you in turn needs to be parallel to each other. Let the ones having more capacity lead the way. Their capacity can be analyzed, only after making way for them and observing him/her. If you have a better skill than him/her, the system in turn will support you in getting in front of them.

Think of the world as "**One Organization with One Objective**", and surviving with the system support.

Do not irritate others, when they start ignoring you.

Every deal is fair, in which no one suffers.

Support of the system can only be realized when you move through situations, this realization can happen at anytime depending on your richness.

"**Fortunate times**" are when some people overcome their fear, this is a part of system mechanism to attain richness.

All wise moves are being incorporated in your mind by observing your surroundings, past experiences and media. All you need is to implement it in your day to day experiences, for the right decisions at a point you come across, for the highest productivity.

88% of your brain is water; it is the combination of other chemicals in the 12% that make it work.

Combinations of information for fuel generation, is what the system requires from you.

The more the information you have the more the combination, in which some have the option to upgrade your productivity. Work on it and use it since the system has given it to you.

"selah"

When one door closes there are 99 doors which open, out of which majority are bigger than this closed door. This is due to your limited sight.

In every game there is a winner and a looser, the looser can in turn be a winner when he attains more strategy, by thinking and testing limits in his future.

"**One who fears defeat can never achieve success**".

This fear can be overcome, by increasing your relationship with the system and finding ways, to overcome defeat.

Combinations of information given to you by the system for maximum output, is what the system requires from you.

Only 11% of the earths surface is feeding 90% of the population on it, increasing it by some percentage can feed all of population.

Or even if you are able to increase the productivity of the 11% itself, you can probably fulfill the total population. It depends on how we plan.

If you have felt the support of the system, you will understand that no one can support you that way.

Every human being who is travelling in the system has an obligation to fuel up the system.

It's not how you know him/her; it's how strong the bond is between both.

Even if you don't share the burden of the needy, do not plant seeds of fear on the needy around you.

"**No rule is good**" if it doesn't produce fuel, while meeting the requirements of the units under it.

Anyone and everyone can produce peace, when they overcome their fear in the right direction.

When you are in the right direction of projection, the constriction which you feel cannot be solved, is the fear which blocks your path of projection. Work in the direction till you are close to the barrier, then with the support from the system, break the block or find a better path to your projection to reach your goal.

It all depends on, how the decision is taken in the right direction with the support from the system.

When the units combine for the right decision/objective, their options for reaching maximum productivity has more probability.

Keep in mind that you are one among superior class of units in the system, who can convert any kind of energy to any other kind of energy with the help of technology and equipments. This cannot be done by the other creatures.

"An Idle mind is the devils workshop, but thinking brain never leaves the mind idle".

Fear is nothing but the work of the opposite force, be strong to dominate them.

When you have past experiences of overcoming fear, you keep growing stronger.

Overcoming fear is always accompanied by the support of the system.

Punishment has to be suffering, for the survival of another's suffering.

The data's you get from other units may not be genuine, but data's you get from the system are.

Any organization will keep growing with happiness and harmony, when it produces peace for the system.

90% of the total sufferings are due to monetary requirement, in which 88% lack its minimum requirement, while the other 2% is worried as they have more than what's required.

Do not react without knowing the genuinity of your data, and if it has the time limit for a situation. Relax; consider better options before the time limit ends for that corresponding situation. Support will come from the system if you are rich.

The governments which meets the native's requirement and which can meet increased immigrant requirements, are the ones with the best policies. Every unit needs the system's fuel for his/her survival. Thus the govt. should generate more in that particular place, as it is the basic requirement for a unit to survive.

Be careful that your output does not contaminate the mind of the surrounding units.

Everyone gains and no one suffers. That is the will of the system.

Every situation, in which fear has been overcome becomes a situation, you can think and laugh about later.

In the Brain, data's given to you are kept above the last data you have received, in the Earth's previous rotation.

You as a unit have the capacity, to arrange the data's according to your priority. You also have the capacity to combine them and create a new concept for a better living environment, and in helping the others around you.

Never take rash decisions, i.e. those decisions without having time to think.

Its not how much you run for money, it's how much you generate peace *(21) while *(21) (*life*) running. It also increases your confidence gained, while having that money with you.

Every information given to you by the system, is for the up- gradation of your combination for better output.

Everything you enjoy is the output of system support, and 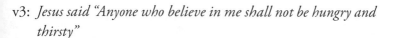 you cannot take it away from the system in your limitless life.

v3: *Jesus said "Anyone who believe in me shall not be hungry and thirsty"*

This is not because your digestive system doesn't function properly.

This means, whatever condition you are in, the system will support you to fill your stomach.

The fear of others along with you growing to higher levels in the hierarchy is the initialization of your destruction.

D

Comfort, Luxury, Health, Wealth, Harmony and Happiness are the by-products of fuel generation.

Another major byproduct is the *(22) support of the system *(22)(*Richness*).

Let those that grow around you grow, don't fear their growth. Give what the system *(23) requires *(23) (*fuel*) and you will also grow automatically with the support of the system.

Unity in the objective along with the wonder support of the system will make the Earth a better place to live in.

For this to be achieved, the tool you have with you is "**Adjustment**", while the tools with the system are "**Adaptation**" and "**Support**".

There exists opportunities of survival in every level of the system, and the system has infinite levels in it.

In all these levels there is an opportunity, which exists to meet your requirements.

As they decipher from astrology, generous people are more probable of getting fooled, as they don't have the tool to measure the intensity of system support.

Energy is not sent out from the system, everything stays within the system and the fact remains that, it is being converted in to many forms of energy to maintain the equilibrium of the system.

The probability of you overcoming fear is high, if you have more faith in the system.

The system doesn't want anyone to suffer; it's the requirements of the rich that makes the system test the weak.

Discovery is the process of understanding the working of the system and its laws.

Invention is the application of discovery, to improve the living comfort for the unit.

Discovery holds the key to Invention.

Invention has to be focused on the requirements of units, as demand is directly proportional to the requirement which in turn defines the inventor's standard.

"selah"

Any group of units which have the same objective and produces peace shall succeed with the support of the system.

Splitting of a group happens due to the growth of fear and the change in direction of a group, in a group.

Sleep is the time, when your mind works with its full capacity.

Your output is what sets your standard. Use of language is like the combinations present in your mind. If the directions are right, the people and the system will support you.

Increase the number of directions or point of view of the people around you in accordance with a standard set in your mind, so that you can think of a direction in which the output doesn't hurt anyone.

No one should say that after drawing a line through a point, that line in the point is the only right. Right has a +_ degree of error. That is the reason why truth can be bent.

Nothing is perfect until there is a mark from the system, which has been limited for us to see; the mark depends on your faith.

You don't know the whole story of what is happening around you, and if there is something you know about someone else's suffering; try helping them in finding peace, so that it can be generated by you.

The quality of generated peace depends on how much time and people you have *(24) spoken to *(24) (*given the output*) on generating your fuel.

In every rotation of the earth as a unit, you will be given choices to make in a situation. All you are left with are some choices. Any choice you make which produces peace is a good decision; the choice where most productivity of peace occurs is the best option.

Braveness is overcoming fear after knowing the consequences of failure.

It's not the brake equipped on a vehicle which helps you avoid accidents. Mostly it's the brake that works, but in some cases the accelerator does help. The steering, the clutch and the gear has its own role at all times.

"Your eyes are limited to see only the reflected part of the light in a visible spectrum".

Along with the objective of a unit in the system, the unit has the capacity to produce peace as much as he/she wants.

It's that productivity, which makes you rich or poor.

Work for increasing your productivity, you will be always supported by the system.

L7: "**Where there is a will, there is a way**"

When the will produces fuel to the system, the way is always supported by the system to make you comfortable.

Your faith in the system increases, when you get the support of the system.

Support of the system, is limited to the person producing the fuel.

The higher the production, the higher the support.

"**Tension**" decreases the capability of your brain, to think of options in a situation.

Time given for thinking in a situation, is always better for arrival of more options. Else project yourself more, for the best option present to give you an output.

Your brain works in accordance with the "**Law of Relativity**".

Discovery is the spine of inventions. Study of discovery is called Science.

What do you think came first, the Chicken or the Egg??.

According to me, the Egg came first. As the evolution happens between generations, the data of the earlier generation is the output for the next generation. As the Egg is the earliest stage of the next generation, it certainly is the Egg. It most probably was some other bird, who laid the Chicken Egg.

Once born, it's only adaptations that occur.

Evolution happens in stages where the initial stage and the final stage exist, and when the transition group gets extinct.

Everything on this planet revolving in its force of gravity is part of your system.

There is everything in the system for everyone. There is no need to draw boundaries within the system, and make others suffers for what you have.

To the Media, kindly do not magnify the worst case scenarios in the system since it plants seeds of fear, in your customers.

It's only when the majority overcome fear, the minority becomes the victims of darkness.

The majority in this particular scenario includes all those who overcome fear, hence there will not be any more minorities or the minorities become strangers to each other.

Let the fuel producers be the majority, with the objective of oneness.

"Comfort is what demand is for". Prioritize your inventions accordingly.

"Achievement of Success" is the combination of information you have received the right way, fed with peace and supported by the system.

The more productive you are, the more important you are to the system.

The more important you are in the system, the richer you become according to the system. Mistakes may/can happen; its how you learn from it, the faults has to be first analyzed.

"Specificity to one subject causes ignorance in others".

In Relation with a chaotic situation, your problems and situations seem small.

Miracles have always been a part of the system support; you are just limited in finding a reason for it.

Every insect in your imagination has a magnified size. How does that feel? This is the primary reason they are small.

Ex: **When you see a blue whale. Does it cause the same feeling as that of a magnified insect, No, Never**.

We humans are the upper level of the food chain.

The system has its own mechanism of increasing the upper level of the food chain, to control the growth of lower level.

The system makes sure that its step of evolution to get bigger is controlled by the system.

In this way, the system always blocks the evolutional steps of non productive units.

"**Good thoughts always give good output**", understand, act and think accordingly.

Do not limit the data to be given to you, by ignoring its opportunities.

Filter the data's you get to remember the good at a present point, and keep the rest for the next point you come across.

Other's judge you on the basis of your output.

You relate with others, to set standards. Any unit which produces maximum peace is the standard unit according to the system, and majority of the units support them.

Those who work for generating fuel shall not fear anything, as they have experienced system support.

Every rotation of the earth sets you different tasks; you in turn are left with the option given to you by your brain.

Opt for the best options which are generated among the most, train your brain to give you more options, by a combination of data's given to you by the system.

The quality of fuel produced by you depends on the quantity of people who are adjusted for the generation, and how many people you have outputted it to.

Without the support of the system you can live, but your life will be complicated.

Never worry about others wealth or growth, appreciate them and observe how his/her productivity happens, and also implement some for your growth.

It's a fear of mind, which creates a barrier between you and situations that produce peace.

When fear is the tool of the opposition, richness is the power to overcome it.

When you can generate peace, you create a stage in your mind where your brain is powered for the system.

In Hierarchy with its different levels of human existence, our thoughts may be on the wealth they hold, which takes them to a higher level. No, "**Wealth**" is just a byproduct of peace generated by the unit.

Everyone hits a peak in the career of his/her life if he/she has system support in order to achieve his/her goals. It's all recorded for your limitless life.

Combine as the fusion happens with the objective of peace production, so that you can enjoy happiness, harmony and system support.

Children are like units which are just below the 10% of space consumed; this 10% are from their parents which is good and peace generating.

"**Civilize**", help the rest get civilized. In the case of those who are uncivilized, accept them and get them corrected.

Water is the basis of life in a unit; this covers about 3/4th of the area and every unit in it.

One who achieves his/her goal without blocking the rest and doesn't plant the seed of fear in others mind, with maximum output, are the best units.

When you have the tool to explore the system, keep observing and try to understand the laws behind it. Knowledge you gain from your observations is not in any way related to your Education, but it helps in understanding the Science behind it.

"**Sacrifice is always associated with something Sacred**". Even the smallest amount of peace generation with your sacrifice, yields a high quality of peace/fuel.

The weak are always tested, so don't be weak. Cling onto the rope of faith, the strength of the rope depends on your productivity.

Only the government policies which can meet the requirements of everyone by keeping them comfortable, shall rule.

Access of development to everyone, has to be implemented.

"**Every cell has a nucleus where the main process, is to happen**".

No one is given permission to judge others by the system. It's their life and they are the ones living it. The one who fairly judges someone for his peace production, is always appreciated by the system.

Support of the system after constant peace production, will be very high.

When you are concentrating on something, there are an infinite number of things happening around you.

"**Tensions are byproducts of fear**". It limits the options given by your brain, at some point in life.

This book conceptualizes, what should be kept in the mind of a literate human while leading a happier life on this system.

"**Languages**" plays a major role in the existence of peace, within its surrounding area.

In some languages, the meaning of a sentence varies by changing the tone of sentence delivery.

Such languages are highly venomous for the production of peace and can lead to, misunderstanding of others.

People who like spreading data with other units from a conversation he/she overheard, without having a complete knowledge of the whole conversation, leads to a change in the meaning of the word you spread.

"Little Knowledge is of much Danger"

Never enjoy another's suffering. Either help him/her or ignore it, if you are dealing with your own suffering.

The only energy emanating, apart from Earths system is that of Sun. Our system has the mechanism of filtering it, before it reaches the Earth's surface.

"Wealth" is the support you have been given in order to enjoy, being a result of your productivity.

Rather than wasting time & energy making other's reputation bad in the society, use the same time and energy for helping the ones who require it. Think of more options for the situation you are in, or the one you are supposed to be in.

A good employer is one who works to reach the objective of any organization, and doing your job as per instructions given in an assigned time period.

No one is perfect, corrective action during a mistake can lead him/her to perfection.

Glass holding water halfway through can be put in different ways.

"selah"

Food is the source of energy for your body, but consumption in excess can cause illness.

The right consumption of food at the right time with the burning of energy, can lead to a healthy body.

T

"Scheme" is the combination of data transactions done between groups/units, to make the unwilling, willing.

"**Corruption**" is a problem, but the bigger problem is the time wasted by others going behind the same.

Apart from the bond between the same blood, there are a lot of other bonds between units.

"**Respect is something that you need to give in order to get it back**".

Likewise, Peace can be enjoyed by those who produce it.

Taking a risk is the procedure to overcome fear and to feel the support of the system, for a producer.

Ex: **95% of those driving at night don't know the number of lines in the symbol of headlight, when in dim.**

Hunger is not actually a requirement of your body during energy deficiency; it is actually a call from your mind, reminding you that you have had food before one rotation at that particular time.

Ex: **85% of the people in a company having lunch at 1 pm, eat at the same time on weekends and holidays.**

Different people have different problems. If you are bound to a person knowing that he/she can be of help to solve his problem, he/she can in turn produce peace.

Opening up one's mind and the problems faced by him/her is explained, only if he/she is confident that you can give them a better option.

"**Respect**" is part of "**Politeness**", Politeness is a part of "**Civilization**" and Civilization on the other hand is a part of "**Productivity**" of fuel and of further development.

You don't know how much others outside our system are developed, so get all the units their basic amenities for survival. Therefore, the time they worry about food or other surviving factors can be used creatively and productively, to get developed and equipped.

No country is developed, since all you are getting to compare is within this small planet in the whole universe.

Do not let the aliens come and take our resources from our systems, using "**Divide and Rule**".

Work for the oneness of human kind, and increase the presence of peace around the system.

Tradition creates a blockage for the civilization, which ends up producing innocent victims.

H

Every subject is a tool, to understand and explore the system. It's not about having the tool with you, it's how you find the opportunity to use it and apply it for the formation of an updated system.

The capacity of a human being to combine the informations received in the past, used in the present and for the better production of fuel in the present and in the future, is the way the system is classified.

"**Freedom**" is the reason for majority of wars.

This is because someone is limiting them from something. That power of limiting someone is only gained, due to development and inventions.

The laws of science are familiar, to the people who have seen it in the nature around with the only problem being, the nature around you differs from another's environment. Everything you see, feel, hear, smell, express and all your activities is the result of a chemical reaction, in which processing out the input and its registration is happening.

It's only when all the equipments for these reactions to take place and its combinations make a complete human being, that the objective of that unit will be different. Even then he/she is obliged to produce peace.

Ex: **Only a person, who has both his legs, will understand the value of it when he/she is paralyzed**.

Therefore people in different parts of the world may not be familiar with the all available *(25) Science in Nature *(25) (*surroundings*), due to the fact that he/she may not be having the same surroundings as the others around them.

"**Scared parent's spoil a child's talent**".

Ex: **You might have seen or mopped a marble floor with water, but the fact remains that, the same water is used to cut marble. This occurs due to the flow of water molecules in the same direction while attacking the same specific point. This, when related to the system shows us that a molecule of the system with same direction in objective to productivity of peace, can break or cut through any barrier of fear.**

Help others with their barriers, in order to help them achieve success.

Once you start thinking about producing peace by taking some decision at some point in your life, then is the time when you must keep thinking of increasing your productivity, in the next similar point of your opportunity in making a decision.

When your brain starts working with the objective of productivity, the system automatically will give you more decision power and then will in-turn hold and lift you up in the hierarchical level of the system, which increases your richness.

I

The force of unity is the result of understanding, adjusting and working for the same objective of every unit in that entity.

The force of unity is infinite in the system. When all the units in the system do the same as is given above, then the objective is the production of peace and development and this will be helped by the support of the system.

"**Unity is Power**" when it is supported by the system and the system support can be expected, only when the unity is for the productivity of peace.

When the feeling of this unity occurs, the opposite force gets suppressed. v4: Jesus Christ told Peter and other Fishermen, *"Come I shall make you fishers of men".*

The man in this particular concept, is always used to share others burden, adjust, understand and act accordingly for maximum peace productivity. This will make you a member of the unit held by them.

None of the dailies tell us the number of people who have successfully reached from a point A to point B. But they are keen to tell us the number of people who have failed.

Ex: **Around the world, if 10's of billions of people travel from A to B. It's only about 10's of thousands of them, meeting with accidents.**

When people read it, they can only see the failures and they are ignorant about the successful.

$$\text{Percentage} = \frac{\text{No of failures}}{\text{Total No of travelers}} \times 100$$

This *(26) magnification *(26)(*equation*) in every sector, keeps the readers mind an apt spot for cultivating the seeds of fear, as they are ignorant about the number lying below.

The news has to be something which motivates the person reading it, and has to make that person proud to be a part of it.

Magnification of failures depresses and demotivates the readers, which in turn blocks creative thought and development in some ways. Magnifying failure is a sin, as it makes the mind of people reading it, ready for cultivating seeds of fear.

When a person with 90% good in him and 10% bad gets criticized and the 10% is magnified ignoring the 90%, people are only aware about that 10% which make the person move into the bad category.

People reading the critic's reports should understand that, he/she is ignorant about the 90% good in him/her.

Any organization or a religion becomes highly productive and efficient, when the combinations of all data's of the units combine for its productivity. Two people are never the same because a couple always gets the same input. Even if they get it, they don't understand it in the same angle. This is the reason why similarity/uniqueness happens in their character.

In the system everything happens as cycles. Circular movement creates circular waves, **"Circle is the Shape of Unity due to gravity"**. Infinite number of lines can be drawn through this same point.

Understand that we are not ruled by papers/currency. In the beginning of all Inventors, money wasn't their main objective. A revolution was what they have seen and set as an objective, and if it is for peace/development of units living in it, was always supported by the system. The wealth you can measure also increases. Only **"Separations"** make different shapes out of a circle.

The geographical barriers are results of opposing forces, but technology and science are highly developed to break the limitations by these barriers. **"Availability of Technology is known as Development"**.

Global warming is a mechanism of the systems for meeting the requirement of rain. It takes more energy now in order to evaporate water, as it is contaminated by pollutants.

Standard of a person is determined by his/her output where the units in the group accept, the 3rd person listening and also accepts the output delivered by that person. It's not the majority or minority which matters, it's only the objective that matters.

The career with the ability of maximum peace generation, are the most paid.

"selah"

Like every product, the production of the fuel has the same law of quantity and quality.

According to system laws, high quality production is highly appreciated by the system.

When every one becomes a part of the systems fuel production, the system develops so that the comfort people are supposed to enjoy in 2050 can be enjoyed in 2020 with maximum happiness, support and growth along with the system. The more developed the more powerful.

It's the combination of the relation between your quality and quantity of productivity, which has developed you into becoming who you are now.

"**Patience**" is the key quality of peace production.

What ever you do you cannot buy time, but you can get it developed faster, so that you can make the energies of the system more efficient.

Every government in the world with low efficiency causes the growth of the illegal, in order to meet the requirements of the units. People who hear your output can be classified into sensitive, they ignore or they react.

In any situation the same person does one of the three.

A group always has this trouble, which can ultimately be reduced by taking the right people with the similar wave length along with you in the journey of life.

Understand the comfort you are enjoying as a result of development. Think ahead, give it a boost.

The comfort you are supposed to enjoy after your death in this limited life can be enjoyed before it, by sitting and working for the objective of peace production.

If you have the projection without supporting the other units around, you might as well not expect the support of the system.

It's your thought of helping the needy, which makes you take the risk.

When you take risks, you can overcome fear and if it's supporting the rest, you will be supported by the system.

This support by the system makes you rich, and gives you a happy, prosperous and peaceful life.

People with "**Fraudulent Characters**" are the "**Barriers**" between "**The Willing and the Needy**".

Ultimately the number of willing reduces and the number of needy increases, which results in the imbalance of equilibrium in the system.

Mother tongue is any language, which a unit relates to while learning another language.

All the top level governing bodies must stop the race; get peace and happiness of all people living in your country. The race thereby gets developed, while also helping others.

Nobody can buy time, but can save time with the help of others and technology.

Majority of inventions are being used, for saving time and reduce its wastage.

As a unit of productivity of fuel, you can overcome the fear of living in the system.

Females have a well fertilized mind, favorable for the growth of seeds of fear.

Understand yourself, fear affects the quality of peace produced. A family with all its units in it produces high quality peace, will survive and succeed for generations.

If the founder has made a cycle of productivity, following which he/she enters the limitless life, the next generation also follows the same cycle. Thence the family becomes stronger.

It's not, for how long you know a person; it's how deep you know him/her.

The system will mostly act closer, to the time limit set by the others. Its only when you give time without reacting, that you feel the support.

N

If "**Heaven**" is the most developed place in the whole universe, its eligibility criteria depends mainly on the quantity and quality of peace produced, in the limited life of that unit in this system.

If you support the system, you can expect support from the system. If you don't get the support for a problem, this is the time the system has access to the future, so it is let to happen. The knowledge you have moreover gained, gets equipped for a future situation which is being forecasted by the system.

Once you get used to this kind of support for a period of time, it shows that you are important to this system. Thus the fear in your mind gets suppressed a little at a time. These are the initial stages of richness.

Once the initial stage is accomplished, get working on increasing your ability of production and the quality of fuel produced with the richness you have gained. Wealth is secondary when system support is primary.

The property of paper is the value of that particular paper, depending on the matter it holds.

Likewise the value of the unit depends on the quantity of system support, this is the result of production of fuel and its quality up-gradation.

"**Sacrificing**" what you don't need to the needy produces fuel, but sacrificing what you need produces high quality fuel, which is always appreciated by the system. Sacrificing what you think you don't need may be required later, but don't worry, if the system supports you and you have faith in the system, it will result in getting you something better as its replacement.

Every coin as two sides but the side which reflects light, makes the decision.

Once you have realized and trusted the support of the system, that is when you go breaking the "**Barrier of Fear**". This is the biggest reason, why the rich get richer and the poor get poorer.

"**Freedom**" is the reason for which fights/wars have happened before; extinction is the result of systemic imbalance caused by species.

You need to set the objective as peace "**the Fuel for the System**" to develop quicker.

By judging others and their faults, one always forgets that there are infinite numbers of lines passing through a point and in your life you come across infinite numbers of the same.

To the fraudulent ones, kindly keep in mind that however you grow and earn, your value in the system remains the same and it in turn moves on to the next generation.

"**Teacher's**" are the ones who bear the tools for nurturing one's talents which is what "**Education**" means, parallely increasing each ones productivity of fuel to the system. It most definitely must be a road leading to richness.

Let the unjust work for the survival of the suffering, if the government is able to provide enough amenities to meet the requirements of every native in that land.

Let the others consume the economy of a respective place, after enough have been consumed by the local natives.

On a brighter note, every deal has a character to give and receive more. The deal of the system is also on a similar level.

When teachers open the right door for their students, there will be no blocks to their success as parallel lines never collide.

It's all about your combination of data's in every point of life, which makes you, what you are now.

If other units support a child in finding the right door, without confusing the child, i.e. not giving them time to explore, observe and process their surroundings, it will thereby begin a production cycle in them.

Ex: **As a child of about 12 yrs of age, my elders used to tell me to watch the news daily. Today on the other hand, children of a similar age are kept away from it**.

"**Being Hasty**" decreases the number of options, since you haven't been given time for your brain to process the rest of the options.

The value of the paper is not the same at all times.

Ex: **If you compare the currency with the highest value today, for purchasing the paintings of Picasso or the First English Bible, you need to pay billions or trillions of that respective currency.**

Natural Calamities are the mechanism of the system to test the weak which can be avoided with the help of technology and system support. It also has a role in maintaining the system balance.

Water is an entity with the most properties and is used as a standard for other entities.

While driving, never let it cross your mind that the ones going slower than you are idiots and faster are maniacs.

Whatever you do without hurting others are "**Neutral**", the same with helping someone in turn "**Generates**". "**Tensions**" cause lot of wastage of energy, so decrease it. Poking your nose into others business is not appreciated by the system. Contaminations are there everywhere, eliminating it leads to perfection.

"selah"

Prioritize your options by calculating the amount of peace produced at a point. Support by a unit, for lifting others burden is always a productive deal.

"**Awareness**" about the objective in the coming era can lead our system forward quicker. News that scares us at unwanted times, plants seeds of fear in other's around.

Mutation is a part of evolution. As has been said before, any species/civilization in balance with the laws of the system will survive.

The testing procedure of the system is high, before the existence of that respective species. When none of them are blocked, there's no sense in waiting for the rest. No definite rule can be put in the system in many cases.

According to western astrology, human character based on the influence of constellation is calculated. The influence of the planet refers to the direction of projection at any point of that person.

Analyze your failures and learn the reason for it, Victory will be waiting for you at the next juncture.

After feeling the support of the system at regular points in life, you start realizing that whatever you do will automatically generate peace. This is when fear is completely eliminated from your mind.

The System has its own laws and mechanisms to keep its balance as it requires fuel for survival.

Hence, plenty of fuel and less wastage can make our system more efficient without its mechanism of phasing out.

Extinction of some civilizations are also due to the same factor of system imbalance.

Keep up the balance with the system for the survival of our future generations.

When fuel is produced by every unit at every point and he/she comes through at a constant point in a day, can thereby result in mass production throughout the system. "**Development**" is related to prevention and prevention is better than cure. Development is the result of invention. "**Inventions**" increases "**Comfort**" and convenience, "**Convenience**" in difficult tasks abolishes or reduces fear of inconvenience.

Inconveniences are caused due to difficulty in having to do complicated tasks. Inconveniences about the task increases wastage due to fear.

For native people struggling to survive, you should know there is a system and it has a lot of places other than your native locality, where you are required and can meet your requirements, all you need is to be ready to adjust initially.

When peace is only present around the system, their confidence level increases to explore rather than being scared to adjust.

Usage of indicators while driving gives convenience, to the ones behind on their way to their destination. Signals when you turn right or left are a convenience for the ones behind you, but switching it on when you don't turn, causes inconvenience to the ones behind.

Any unit has the capacity to produce fuel only if it is generated at a lower level. Higher levels can be accessed by you, as many units have done before and also in the present.

The barrier towards producing fuel is "**Fear**" of mind; it's only when you overcome it, that your production capability increases.

The word "**Combination**" is derived from the word combine and they are directly proportional to "**Production**". The word "**Combine**" refers to a "**Combination of Units**".

It's only when the combination of ideas happens, the number of units increasing the probability of getting the right options due to higher number of options. If and only if the units in the combination have the same objective that is parallel to the system, you can always expect a system support.

A Profession with the ability of high productivity are also paid well.

Never compromise on convenience with currency, when inconvenience causes trouble.

Every coin has two sides; make sure that the side you focus on is the right side, whilst the other side always remains in darkness.

As you increase your level of production, the system takes you to its higher level of hierarchy where, conveniences increase so as to decrease trouble.

Its all you object for and how the system supports you.

Your skill of production always has to be without hurting the next, for that you need to know the limits of the others behind or around you. If you observe it, there will be a path where you can mutually go hand in hand with the production of fuel. The problems with calculated moves are that, you do not know the future situation this calculated move leads to.

Life is a complexity of simple stuff; it all depends on how you develop that complexity.

Having a fraudulent character is the fault of one's parents, no point blaming fraudulence.

System prevents the growth of fear in a unit, citing vaccine as an example.

"selah"

When your mind is given a small amount of fear and you learn to overcome it, is like an antibody getting strength to overcome the next attack. Your mind also works in the same way.

As you proceed in getting these vaccinations, for all kinds of fear given to you by the system your path towards richness is guaranteed by the system.

"Fear" is the **"villain"** in the system. The ones that overcome it become heroes.

When worry is the outcome of fear, richness is the outcome of system support.

The term systematic refers to any action, continuing at a regular interval to meet the requirements of the system to run. **"Systematic"** will always be associated with **"Success"**. According to the system, developed countries have successful systematic ways to keep up the balance with the system.

Rules are/will be/should be to keep this balance with the system.

Punishing an innocent is the failure of this rule, according to the system.

Everything happens for a reason, "**Reasons**" are the mechanism of the system to equip you or help you to gain richness.

Conveniences are the result of troubles due to inconvenience.

Before and at present, development can break the barrier of inconvenience which in turn reduces fear of inconvenience, in the units suffering due to it.

Remember, every person classify/filter others by the value the other person gives to that amount, since you cannot measure the main product you can only measure the by product.

"**Generosity**" is one of the components of the production reactions, where "**Patience**" and "**Forgiveness**" also participate.

It is the responsibility of every unit to keep up with the balance of the system, while producing fuel for it.

No one likes cutting their comfort for the rest; you also will probably be thinking on the same wavelength. Hence, make sure you are not the one, the rest are cutting their comforts for.

There are many kinds of bonds in the system, its that bond between units which holds the capacity of data transfer. Compromise on anything, except that which affects your production or its quality.

Oneness with mutual benefits with the system and with one objective can speed things up, even if time can't be bought.

Every experience and data you get while sharing the burden of others, are like the vaccines for you against the fear of such situations.

When many of such vaccines are functioning, it's the path to richness. There is a time for everyone, what counts are the produced quantity and quality at that time when you were in the system.

The "**Lesser**" you have the fear of tomorrow, the "**Stronger**" you are today. Heaven is the most developed with a 100% efficiency of that system, but the entry is restricted by the amount and quality of your production.

"**Currency**" is always associated with "**Current**", as its only property is that it flows and every unit divides its path, in exchange of the unit's requirement. The money spent by a unit will be saved in some percentage on every level he/she has spent it. When you get something worth, with the money you have spent and some unit of every level saved out of it, it's also a way of producing peace.

The more stagnant the money you have, more the chances of fear growing in your mind.

Money is a medium used to overcome the fear of inconvenience by exchanging it, so as to make the same convenience with the help of technology or the resources of others.

When you think something has happened. The reason in your mind may not be the reason for that happening.

System gives you opportunity to produce peace in its every rotation. All you need is to see the opportunity given by it.

Even a small nut has its place in the system. It's hard to find richness by those units who fear taking risks, in producing fuel for the system.

Its because they have trees of fear in their minds. For those who achieve richness, money is like a medicine to cut the fear of inconvenience, by getting convenience in exchange for this medium.

What you output through your mouth or doings, is the correlation of your brain and mind. Mind filters the processed output from your brain; this process is similar to the quality checking of products from a machine/organization. When your mind is filled with fear and negative energy/force, it passes only the brains output, of the similar kind of fear.

But when the mind is filled with richness and knowledge about system support, it passes the brains output of the similar kind.

The advantage of a rich mind is, their output and doings produces peace, its fuel generating, they will be supported by the medium to cut the barrier of inconveniences and they will be having their system support in every action.

When constantly keeping the seed of richness in your mind, it grows and becomes a "**Tree of Faith**". When this tree starts yielding, whatever you do the system makes sure that the situations automatically gets setup in such a way that, the constant production capacity gets increased.

An open mind always attracts other units to solve their problem which in turn produces fuel to the system. Attack is the best defense but it cannot break all defenses. It's the bond between units which makes the other's conveniences/resources yours in some situations. When the system has more fuel, the Earth is not going to rotate faster, only the reaction of developments gets faster.

Remember, "**Ones Right is not the Only Right**". Understand your deficiency in knowing what others are thinking/facing. All you can do is to avoid the system testing you; it also depends on your richness or objective of getting it. Be proud of overcoming fear, the barrier towards production.

K

Childhood is the time when you explore around you, without bothering for your survival.

Education has its own limitation as each student is unique, but education can to some extent get them to set their objective, while producing peace.

Never stress or strain a child in the name of education, every unit has his/her inborn right to explore around him/her.

All education can or should do, is to find the talents of every student and equip him/her with the tools required by them, to explore the same talent. They are also taught not to block anyone from reaching their goal while getting system support, and setting up the objective of peace production.

The technology you are enjoying now is the combination of replication of system/nature around you. The value given to you by the system is inversely proportional to the value you give to the money.

There is a reason why everyone around you is present around you. "**Greediness**" is another byproduct of fear.

Cut all the trees of fear in your mind and cultivate/plant the seeds of richness, which may take time to yield. The younger the seeds are when planted, the faster it gives a yield of richness.

Without output in a situation is neutral according to the system. "**Politeness**" is directly proportional to receiving respect and civilization.

Many outputs continuously reduce the attention of others around you. Start generating peace at every point you are in, in every rotation in the system and keep upgrading them to find the path of richness. It's always the relation with something visible which is being used to develop science.

Fuel is what everything including the system requires for its running, but the fuel needs keep changing in every level of the system.

"**Energy**" in the system never goes out of the system; the wastage of energy is where there is the conversion of one energy to another, while some energy cannot be used. In other words, the systems classification of units depending on their quality and quantity of production by a person, highly verify the opportunities given by the system for their production.

You measure everything with what you can see; your deeper accessibility is limited by the system.

A healthy person always needs earthly stuff, if it affects the system balance/richness; it causes diseases for that corresponding person.

Such combination of data's which affect system balance, causes the system to use the mechanism of diseases, in order to limit the units needs.

Calculated moves may fail but the system support will never. If you feel that the system support has failed, then what you have to understand is that either you are being tested since you haven't produced enough. If you have already achieved richness, then understand that the system has its own way of knowing what happens after a couple or few rotations which you are limited to see. The system for a fact knows about it, so it has made its move looking at the projections after a few rotations.

Breaking the barrier of fear of mind, within one's mind is by using the "**Tool of Faith**".

Fear affects the quantity of your production.

"**Knowledge is power**" makes a valid argument, only when you have an opportunity with that to produce fuel. "**Anger**" is the excessive burning of fuel which reduces your efficiency of production. Higher the amount of money you deal with, the higher are the chances of producing fuel, as money is what the majority require.

The value of money increases as you go down the levels of system hierarchy. Every human being is a needy but their needs vary. "**Circle**" is the shape of the system, as the binary digit "**0**" is to a computer.

Ex: **Touching water contained in a bucket when stagnant can make ripples for approximately 20 seconds; this is a visible example of energy conversion with that touch**.

Likewise, the number of invisible waves produced by each reaction in your brain can produce infinite invisible waves all around you. "**Depression**" is a result of a strong barrier of fear within your mind. Overcome it, by experiencing the support of the system.

Depending on each product's quality and quantity, the system classifies all units respectively. The higher the level you are in the hierarchy, the faster you get your needs fulfilled by the system.

If you are against this production, the system tests you for meeting the requirement of the units, in the higher level of the system hierarchy.

Every place has its own capabilities and weaknesses. The directions of development should focus in this direction, considering the capabilities of those places.

Inconveniences faced by the natives living in a particular place under a rule, show the weaknesses or incapability of the units governing that place.

I am writing this book as an observer and as a unit looking towards limitless life. As a part of the system, I would like to make you clear about the characters, laws and the system mechanism and also keep the oneness in the objective of all units in the system.

Increase the productivity of fuel in the system and speed up the development, in order to break the fear of inconvenience around the system.

Every method of peace generation differs according to the situations you are or the others are in. After reading this book, the units who have already achieved richness should certainly upgrade his/her skills, while others must try achieving it.

"**Currency**" was the solution for the inconvenience faced by the people during the time of "**Barter System**"; it's not what is ruling the system.

Expect nothing from a unit while you share its burden, as its action has a high value according to the system and expectation from that unit may lead to dissatisfaction.

The solution to your entire problems is being blocked by the fear developed in you, due to the inputs fed.

"selah"

Breaking that barrier of fear can only be attained by faith and system support, which is the result of the quality and quantity of fuel generated according to the system, in every point you come across.

Every government should upgrade itself for satisfying the needs of everyone inside, whilst you have monetary abundance. **"Where there is demand there will always be supply"**, it's this relation with convenience of supply that is called development.

The more fuel you produce, the more are your chances of getting system support.

Analyze your past and update your present in order to achieve a pleasant future. It's not the unit you supported rewarding you, it's the system which rewards you as per your needs.

Once you achieve richness don't waste your time in being negative and passing the processed output from your brain, through your mind's tree of fear.

The more you have access to units, the more are the data's given to you by the system, how you utilize it also matters. Use it to generate fuel by helping the other units who have access to overcome the fear, in a given situation.

Fertilizing the seeds of richness with production of peace in all the possible points you come across, helps you get faster and finer yield.

"Education" has to be the mechanism in achieving the same.

Availability of everything, everywhere and for every citizen is sound; so that he can get everything he needs, without much effort or making a dent in his/her savings. That is what the Government needs to target.

Life is a combination of data's, which you are equipped at any point in your life.

Do not quit, there is always an invisible door yet to open, keep your faith till the end. If you're not rich, modify your thoughts to get the support of the system.

"**Support**" is always given to good units who never waste opportunities. Generate fuel and get your seat reserved in the upper levels of the system. Tests do occur, but do what you must do, produce fuel in those situations.

Once you are in the list of the rich, the system will take care of you until you change your direction of projection, and cause faults in production.

Until you feel richness keep your plans on hold and work for production. With the support of the system every plan of yours is taken care of. Achieve it before you act.

Don't go poking around looking for the negatives in a unit/organization. Ask the system for your requirements and when each unit starts producing fuel in the system, the load the government bears will decrease.

No one gains anything, finding faults in others.

As the yield of richness is received, thank the system for the support you have enjoyed in hard times.

Always increase the number of options at every point, so that you have a better chance of increasing your productivity.

Always work on increasing your productivity, rather than affecting other units.

The faster you produce, the faster will be the growth of your mind's seeds of richness.

The word "**Love**" is complicated in this era/now. "**Richness**" can demolish the tree of fear and can prevent your mind from growing it again.

Everyone works for happiness and for meeting their needs. Males are the raw materials and females are the machines for the production of the product. Children on the other hand are opportunities given to you, to correct your past mistakes.

Inconveniences caused by you to other units, are negative for production.

The more you adjust, the more you understand a unit.

Even if anyone tries to harm you and you are still able to generate peace, the system will not let it do any harm.

Money is a current and the speed of development is high where the flow is high.

Stagnating money is wasting opportunities; there are people who are suffering because of its shortage.

Hard work is different from dedicated work, dedicated work leads to success. This seems to look like hard work or vise-versa but in the case of dedicated work, you don't feel stress or strain.

Don't underestimate anyone, for anybody can show you the path towards richness.

Understand yourself, the space you and the other units you deal with need, in-order to mark limits.

Everything you come across is the reason for data transfer by the system. It is up to you on how they are combined for production.

After achieving richness, every data you get will be a tool for the next point. This happens only after the tree grows and yields a couple of times.

Every move has its own pros and cons, the options with more pros according to the laws of the system, should be executed.

The World will be a better place tomorrow, if you do what you have to do now!!!!

By

J.A. Thomas

GLOSSARY

Unit - *Refers to any individual.*

Literate - *Refers to anyone who can READ, WRITE and THINK.*

Heaven - *Refers to the most developed place which exists outside our system.*

God - *Ruler of Heaven*

System - *Earth*

Fuel - *Peace*

Generating/Production of fuel - *Peace can be generated by helping others, so they enjoy what you have generated/produced.*

Richness - *It is the mechanism of the system to classify people according to their peace generating capacity, quality of peace generated given the opportunities and the importance of every individual according to the system.*

J.A. Thomas

'Selah' – *A Hebrew word used as a biblical reference translates to STOP AND THINK.*

This book supports the existence of aliens, as we have explored less than the 5% of the Milky Way.